THIRST FOR

THE CAFOD/ CHRISTIAN AID
LENT BOOK 2008

Chris Chivers • **Anthea Dove**
Mary Grey • **Robert Kaggwa**
Nicholas Sagovsky • **Hugo Slim**

THIRST FOR LIFE

Reflections on the
Scripture Readings for Lent 2008

First published in Great Britain in 2007 by

CAFOD
Romero Close
Stockwell Road
London SW9 9TY

Christian Aid
35 Lower Marsh
London SE1 7RL

Darton, Longman and Todd Ltd
1 Spencer Court
140–142 Wandsworth High Street
London SW18 4JJ

ISBN 0 232 52721 0

Bible quotations are taken predominantly from the New Jerusalem Bible, published and copyright © 1985 by Darton, Longman and Todd Ltd and Doubleday, a division of Random House, Inc.

Note: the Hebrew numbering of the Psalms is used. From Psalm 10 to 147 this is ahead of the Greek and Vulgate numbering which is used in some psalters.

Cover photo: Caroline Irby/CAFOD
Cover design: Leigh Hurlock

Text designed and produced by Sandie Boccacci
Set in 9.5/13pt Palatino
Printed and bound in Great Britain by
Athenaeum Press Ltd, Gateshead

Contents

About the authors   vii

Introduction   Brendan Walsh   ix

**Ash Wednesday
to Saturday after
Ash Wednesday**   Nicholas Sagovsky   2

First week of Lent   Nicholas Sagovsky   10

Second week of Lent   Anthea Dove   24

Third week of Lent   Robert Kaggwa   38

Fourth week of Lent   Hugo Slim   52

Fifth week of Lent   Mary Grey   66

**Holy Week and
Easter Sunday**   Chris Chivers   80

About CAFOD   97

About Christian Aid   99

About the authors

Chris Chivers is Canon Chancellor of Blackburn Cathedral. He writes for *Cape Times, Church Times*, *The Tablet* and *Church of England Newspaper,* is a regular presenter of Daily Service on BBC Radio 4, a published composer, a trustee of USPG, and the author of several books. He was formerly Precentor both of St George's Cathedral, Cape Town and Westminster Abbey.

Anthea Dove works with a resource centre for the disadvantaged in her home town of Whitby, North Yorkshire. A retired teacher and experienced retreat giver, she spent four years as a member of the ecumenical community at Hengrave Hall in Suffolk. Her many books include *The Mass and Mary Brown* and *To Calvary with Mary* (Columba).

Mary Grey was D. J. James Professor of Pastoral Theology at the University of Wales, Lampeter, and is now Professorial Research Fellow, St Mary's University, Twickenham. Her most recent book is *To Rwanda and Back: Liberation spirituality and reconciliation* (DLT). Her many other books include *Redeeming the Dream* (SPCK), *The Outrageous Pursuit of Hope – Prophetic Dreams for the 21st Century* (DLT) and *Sacred Longings: Ecofeminist theology and Globalization* (SCM).

Robert Kaggwa, a member of the Society of Missionaries of Africa, studied in his native Uganda, France, Germany and Rome. He taught theology at the Missionary

Institute London (Middlesex University) and was research associate at the Von Hügel Institute, Cambridge. He is now chaplain and part time lecturer in theology at Roehampton University in South West London.

Nicholas Sagovsky is Canon Theologian at Westminster Abbey. He was previously Dean and Director of Studies in Theology, Clare College, Cambridge, William Leech Professorial Research Fellow, Newcastle University, and Professor of Theology and Public Life, Liverpool Hope University College. He is the author of several books and articles on ecumenism, theology and justice.

Hugo Slim was till recently chief scholar at the Centre for Humanitarian Dialogue in Switzerland. Previously he was Reader in Internationalism at Oxford Brookes University, on the council of Oxfam GB and worked for Save the Children UK and the United Nations in Sudan, Ethiopia, Morocco and the Palestinian Territories. He is the author of *Killing Civilians: Method, Madness and Morality in War* (Hurst).

'Ask and it will be given to you; search and you will find; knock and the door will be opened to you.'

This is God's extraordinary promise. In a broken world, scarred by suffering and brutality, we are asked to trust in God's unconditional love for each and every one of us.

In Lent, we prepare for Easter, when Christians celebrate the rising from the dead of Jesus, by prayer and fasting and the giving of alms to the poor.

We turn to God in prayer, believing that those who suffer the most are those closest to God's heart. We act to repair the world that we have made, a world full of wonders and of horrors.

These scripture readings show us a God who hungers and thirsts for justice. They have opened the eyes of men and women throughout history, enabling them to see their preciousness in the eyes of God, and giving them the strength to claim a different future for themselves and their children.

But as Nicholas Sagovsky reminds us in his reflection for the first Thursday of Lent, although we are assured that if we search we shall find, we are not told what we shall find. We know that so often people don't get the things they pray for. It can be hard to believe that God has something better in store. But that is what Jesus teaches.

In Lent we turn to prayer. We try to live as simply as we can, mindful of the needs of others, celebrating and relishing the good things of creation. We seek, we knock on the door, yet we do not know what lies at the end of the Lenten journey. But our hope is in our heavenly Father who's love for us is beyond imagining.

Brendan Walsh

THIRST FOR LIFE

THE CAFOD/ CHRISTIAN AID
LENT BOOK 2008

Nicholas Sagovsky

Ash Wednesday to Saturday after Ash Wednesday

Ash Wednesday

What Matters to God is the Real 'You'

Jl 2:12–18; Ps 51; 2 Cor 5:20–6:2; Mt 6:1–6, 16–18

> 'When you pray, go to your private room and, when you have shut your door, pray to your Father who is in that secret place, and your Father who sees all that is done in secret will reward you.' (Matthew 6:5–6)

Being honest with ourselves is a constant battle. We say 'How are you?' but we don't really want to hear the answer; we tell people we're 'fine' when we aren't. We are told that if we are going to get on in life we must present ourselves in the best possible light. Politicians and presenters are trained to answer that things are going 'fine' when they are not. Most of our media don't want us to ask too many hard questions. When the news presents us with some of the painful realities, it can all get too much, and we escape at the push of a button.

There's something strangely comforting (that is to say, strengthening) about the beginning of Lent. It's a time for facing up to reality. On Ash Wednesday the sign of the cross is traced on our forehead with the ashes from last years' palm crosses. Just once in the year we are told to

'Remember you are dust and to dust you shall return' – but that's the truth about our everyday lives. During Lent we have an opportunity to face up to what it means to be mixed-up human beings in a world where is almost always safer to hide the real 'me'. Not many of us have time to go off into the desert or on retreat, but we can usually find a quiet place to be alone – and we can usually find some time to be honest with ourselves in the presence of God. We can be open to the gift of prayer. Jesus warns against outward demonstrations of piety intended to impress other people, to deceive ourselves and God. Lent is a time to explore more honestly, with God, who I am and what it means to be alive in the world he has created.

Thought for the day
As humans, we practise deception every day. God never deceives: he knows us and loves us for what we are.

Prayer
O Lord, I am frightened that if I were honest with myself about the way I am and the way the world is, I couldn't bear it. Yet you know me and you put up with me all the time. Please give me courage this Lent not to hide from you and not to hide from the needs of other people in your world. Amen

A Clear Choice

Dt 30:15–20; Ps 1; Lk 9:22–25

> *Then to all he said, 'If anyone wants to be a follower of mine, let him renounce himself and take up his cross every day and follow me.'* (Luke 9:23)

The Christian life begins with a clear choice. When we are baptized, whether as a child or an adult, the promise is made that we shall turn away from sin and follow Christ. We are baptized into – that is to say we become one with – Christ. In the same way Jesus' ministry began with a clear choice. He chose to come to John the Baptist to be baptized by him. That set the direction for his ministry, but every day he had to renew his commitment to the way on which he was being called, especially when it became the way to Jerusalem; the way of the cross.

In Luke's Gospel, Jesus reminds us that there is sure to be a cost to this discipleship. Just as Jesus took the twelve to Jerusalem, where they would all suffer, so, when we commit ourselves to follow him, we commit ourselves to accept the suffering that is sure to come at some time in our lives.

For a Christian, the fundamental choice has been made. We have said 'Yes' to Jesus Christ and have committed ourselves to follow him. However, what he asks of his disciples is a daily re-commitment to follow him in the circumstances of this day. When we set out with Christ, we have no idea where he will take us or what will happen to us in our life. Every day is different and each day has new challenges. The only question that really matters is, 'Will you be my disciple today?'

Thought for the day

For the follower of Jesus, the only question that really matters is, 'Will you be my disciple today?'

Prayer

Lord Jesus Christ, I thank you for the gift of baptism. Please grant me the grace to choose your way in what you ask of me today. But not only to me: I pray for those who today are called to be your disciples in hunger, persecution, through natural disaster or in sickness. May they have grace to choose your way in what you ask of them. Amen

A Time for Fasting

Is 59:1–9; Ps 51; Mt 9:14–15

> *Jesus replied, 'Surely the bridegroom's attendants would never think of mourning so long as the bridegroom is still with them? But the time will come for the bridegroom to be taken away from them, and then they will fast.'* (Matthew 9:15)

Jesus makes it clear that the short time he has with his disciples is not a time for fasting. At this stage of his ministry there's a party atmosphere. He speaks of himself as the bridegroom. He doesn't challenge people to be more religious but to take delight in what God is doing now. The poor people understand this very well.

Jesus recognises that there will be a time for fasting. He isn't against fasting – but it should be at the right time and in the right way. The Church teaches that Lent is a time for fasting – not because Christ has gone away from us but because we so easily lose touch with him and with his priorities.

In much of the western world, Christians hardly fast at all. This is strange, because in the wealthy nations overeating is a major problem. We could do with a bit more fasting. Amongst the world's wealthy nations, obesity and diabetes are on the increase, while in the poor nations children become sick and die through lack of nourishing food.

It may be that in wealthy nations we shall re-learn how

to fast from churches in those countries where there are serious shortages of food but Christians haven't forgotten that fasting is part of the Christian life. We shan't really know how to fast until we are hungry for what the poor have to teach us about joy in the presence of Jesus.

Thought for the day

There's more to fasting than going without fast-food.

Prayer

Teach me, O lord, when and how to fast. Show me the links between my greed and the need of those who go hungry. And give me strength to do something – however little, and however much a first step – about it today. Amen

The day sacred to Yahweh

Is 58:9–14; Ps 86:1–6; Lk 5:27–32

> *If you refrain from trampling the sabbath,*
> *And doing business on the holy day,*
> *If you call the sabbath 'Delightful',*
> *And the day sacred to Yahweh 'Honourable',*
> *If you honour it by abstaining from travel,*
> *And from doing business and from gossip,*
> *Then you shall find your happiness in Yahweh*
> *And I will lead you triumphant over the heights*
> *of the land.*
>
> (Isaiah 58:13–14)

This is the first sabbath day of Lent. Many Jews around the world today will have lit lamps in their house and enjoyed a family meal last night. Today they won't go to work, they will make a priority of attending synagogue, they won't take long journeys and they won't go shopping. In a 24/7 society that's not easy – but for a Jew it is part of their very identity. It can only be done if one has the right kind of job and family structure is geared for it.

In a 24/7 society the people who find it hardest to keep the sabbath are the poor. If they have work, they probably don't have a choice about when they work, or when they rest – if they do rest – and when they can get to church.

If the wealthy don't value the sabbath for themselves, they certainly won't value it for the poor, who don't have the power to observe the sabbath as they may wish. A generous Christian faith will value the observing of one sacred day a week not just for myself and for my family, but for my neighbour of another faith. Can we construct a society in which people are free to observe one holy day a week – whether Friday, Saturday or Sunday – in accord with the teachings of their faith? Yes, if we care enough about the teaching that there should be one day a week sacred to God.

Thought for the day

Love for my neighbour includes love for my neighbour's sabbath.

Prayer

Lord, you have placed us in a world where there are seven days in a week, one of which is to be, above all others, sacred to you. May we learn how, in a 24/7 world, we can observe one day in a week as sacred; may we be sensitive to the need for that sacred rest in the lives of others. Amen

Nicholas Sagovsky

First Week of Lent

First Sunday of Lent

One Good Turn

Gen 2:7–9, 3:1–7; Ps 51; Rom 5:12–19; Mt 4:111

> '*As by one man's disobedience many were made sin-ners, so by one man's obedience many will be made righteous.*' (Romans 5:18)

'One good turn', we say, 'deserves another.' The New Testament readings for today talk about a decisive 'turn' in human history through the ministry of Jesus, which undoes the 'bad' turn of Adam and Eve in the dim and mythical past. The story of Adam and Eve's 'turn' away from God is the story of the challenge each of us makes to the God-given limitations of our human existence. We are not satisfied with the way things are, and we think we can rearrange them better. Unfortunately, there are certain things about being human – suffering, death and the competitive instinct for self-preservation – which we cannot change no matter how we rage against them.

Paul presents Jesus Christ as one who of his own free will accepted the human situation without ever being corrupted by it. He accepted the role he had been given within the human drama, a role that led him to his own annihilation. In him, the 'bad' turn of Adam and Eve was decisively reversed. His response to God's will for him was one of open, undefended acceptance. The instinct for self-preservation from suffering and death was subsumed in peaceful acceptance that God would preserve him through the terrifying ordeal that lay ahead.

In that acceptance lies the 'one good turn' that 'deserves another'. When Jesus refused to turn from the path God had set before him, a new era dawned in human history. A Christian is someone who accepts that the 'one good turn' which determined the path Jesus took deserves another. In penitence, we turn, and, for us too, the new era dawns.

Thought for the day
To turn, in the sense of 'turning to God', is also to 'return'.

Prayer
Lord, when you took the path of costly obedience, there was a sense in which that was done for me. You have opened for me a 'new and living way' to return to God. Give me strength and courage, I pray, to follow your way to the end. Amen

God with us – God in my neighbour

Lv 19:1–2, 11–18; Ps 19; Mt 25:31–46

> *Then the virtuous will say to him in reply, 'Lord, when did we see you hungry and feed you; or thirsty and give you drink? When did we see you a stranger and make you welcome; naked and clothe you; sick or in prison and go to see you?'* (Matthew 31:37)

Today's reading from Leviticus runs through some of the commandments. When the people are gathered before Moses, God gives a series of instructions that are to be kept by the whole people. Some of them speak very directly to us: you must not steal nor deal deceitfully or fraudulently with your neighbour; you must not swear falsely, profaning the name of your God; you must not exploit or rob your neighbour; you must not keep back the labourer's wage until next morning; you must not be guilty of unjust verdicts; you must not exact vengeance; you must love your neighbour as yourself. If you want to be holy, you must treat your neighbour with justice and love. Yahweh's people are to be like Yahweh. 'Be holy, for I, Yahweh your God, am holy.' 'I am Yahweh' comes back again and again, like a refrain, through the list of the commandments.

Matthew's Gospel approaches things differently. Jesus tells a parable about all the nations being gathered before the Son of Man. The people are to be separated out like sheep and goats, according to the way they have behaved. The virtuous are to be placed on his right hand because: 'I was hungry and you gave me food; I was thirsty and you gave me drink; I was a stranger and you made me welcome; naked and you clothed me, sick and you visited me, in prison and you came to see me.' They are surprised by the way the Son of Man, who is also Christ the King, speaks of himself as present in the hungry, the thirsty, the stranger, the naked, the sick, the imprisoned. They had missed the point that he is Immanuel, 'God with us'– 'God in my neighbour'.

Thought for the day
Holiness begins with how I treat my neighbour – today.

Prayer
Lord, open my eyes to see who is my neighbour; open my heart to love my neighbour; open my life to the generous holiness that finds you in my neighbour's need. Amen

Forgive us our debts as we have forgiven those who are in debt to us.

Is 55:10–11; Ps 34; Mt 6:7–15

> *'And forgive us our debts, as we have forgiven those who are in debt to us.'* (Matthew 6:12)

Modern societies run on debt. Nations borrow so they can develop their infrastructure. Young people borrow so they can buy somewhere to live or set up a business. Students borrow so they can study and obtain qualifications. Debt isn't a problem to us – provided we can repay it when we need to. In a demand-led culture, we are encouraged all the time to borrow more than we can repay. Credit card debts spiral out of control and we borrow yet more to pay them off. We want to live at a level beyond what we can actually afford.

When debt gets out of control it becomes a kind of bondage. We are never free from the nightmare, and when the pressure is on – perhaps through the threat of the bailiffs or the loan shark's men, or the representatives from the World Bank, coming round – the need to repay the money blights every aspect of our lives. This is why there was such an emphasis on 'dropping the debt' for the poorest nations in the Jubilee 2000 and Make Poverty History campaigns. Some remarkable progress was made. For some of the most highly indebted nations debts were remitted (though we need to check to what extent headline-grabbing promises have been delivered).

But the unremitting pressure of indebtedness continues to blight lives in both wealthy and in poor nations.

Debts can usually be rescheduled or in part remitted, but not always. There may be very little we can do to help someone who is in debt – though in the UK there are charities like Citizens Advice Bureaux and Zacchaeus 2000 who can give help and advice. There are, however, debts that can and should be remitted, and there may be situations where we can play our part in liberating others caught in the terrible chains of debt.

Thought for the day
Is there anyone whose debt to me blights their life? What can I do to help set them free?

Prayer
Show me, Lord, where I have received liberating generosity from others. Show me, too, where I can and should be generous in liberating others. Please help me to live with the generosity of spirit that forgives others their debts to me. Amen

The Sign of Jonah, God's unlikely Messenger

Jon 3:1–10; Ps 51; Lk 11:29–32

> *'For just as Jonah became a sign to the Ninevites, so will the Son of Man be to this generation.'*
>
> (Luke 11:30)

Jonah was a prophet who didn't give a sign. When Jesus talks about 'the sign of the prophet Jonah', he means that Jonah himself was a sign. Not a very impressive sign. For those who knew the story in the Hebrew Bible there was a sign in his three days spent in the belly of the fish before he was vomited on to the shore: a most undignified way for a failed prophet to arrive back safely. Yet Jesus compares himself to the great prophet Jonah!

Jesus' primary concern is, however, with what Jonah meant to the Ninevites. Jonah arrived on the outskirts of the vast city warning that, unless its inhabitants repented, in forty days Nineveh would be overthrown. God spoke to them through the most reluctant prophet in the Old Testament and they responded. Led by the king, throughout the whole of their society, they repented. No disaster came upon Nineveh but Jonah was mightily indignant. He reckoned he had wasted his time.

Why couldn't the people of Jesus' own generation see in him a prophet like the prophet Jonah? His message was far more hopeful than the message of Jonah; unlike Jonah he wasn't a reluctant conscript to the ranks of the prophets. People hear what they want to hear, and, if they don't want to hear, one of the strategies is to rubbish the messenger: he comes from Nazareth; he's not properly trained or qualified; he doesn't know what he's talking about. We are not told what it was that made the Ninevites take Jonah seriously. Perhaps they already half-knew how bad things really were. They responded to the message, even when God sent one of his most unlikely messengers.

Thought for the day
Are there things that we half-know are seriously wrong with our society? If so, who's pointing them out?

Prayer
Lord, I want to hear what you have to say to our society. I don't need a sign but I do need help to listen and to respond in the right way to your unlikely messengers. Amen

Search and you will find

Est 4:1–3; 5:12–14; Ps 138; Mt 7:7–12

> *'Ask and it will be given to you; search and you will find; knock and the door will be opened to you.'*
>
> (Matthew 7:7)

'Ask and it will be given to you; search and you will find; knock and the door will be opened to you.' Just what are we being promised here? At a superficial glance, this looks like a promise about getting what we want. All we have to do is pray for it. But we know that's too simple.

We are told that if we ask we shall receive; if we search we shall find; if we knock the door will be opened. We are not told what will be given to us, what we shall find, or how the door will be opened. The point is to bring our requests, our searching, our longing to God, who is our heavenly Father.

Of course it is hard to believe, when we don't get the things that we pray for, especially when we pray for others, that God has something better in store. But that is what Jesus teaches. Paul says that we don't know what we should pray for but the Spirit helps us in our weakness (Rom 8:26). Only when we really ask do we discover what it is God wants to give us; only when we really search do we discover what it is God wants us to find; only when we really knock is the door opened in the way God wants.

If we, with all our human weakness and contradictions, know how to be generous with our children, God certainly knows how to be generous with us. To make the point, Jesus could well have said, 'Is there a man among you who would hand your son a stone when he asked for a stone? Or would hand him a snake when he asked for a snake?'

Thought for the day
'Is there a person among you who would hand your child a snake when she asked for a snake?'

Prayer
Lord, in my prayers, let me ask, let me seek, let me knock – and then let me receive what you give, discover what you want me to find, accept the way and the time in which new doors open for me. And let me be thankful. Amen

No more cycles of violence!

Ez 18:21–28; Ps 130; Mt 5:20–26

> *'So then, if you are bringing your offering to the altar*
> *and there remember that your brother has something*
> *against you, leave your offering there before the altar,*
> *go and be reconciled with your brother first, and then*
> *come back and present your offering.'*
>
> (Mattthew 5:23–24)

The Sermon on the Mount is often quoted as a high-point of religious teaching, even by people who are not followers of Jesus. When we look at it more closely, it can seem exaggerated and extreme. Here Jesus warns that if we are angry with our brother we'll end up in court, and if we insult our brother we shall answer for it 'in hell fire'. He warns that anger can lead to assault, and injury can lead to murder, and murder – especially within the family – can lead to hellish remorse.

This is teaching given, or noted down, in shorthand, but we don't have to read very far between the lines to learn from it. Jesus isn't talking about every situation of breakdown. Sometimes there's very little we can do about a breakdown in relations between communities and our work for reconciliation has to be long-term. Here he is talking about a feud with a brother – though a brother could mean anyone within the Christian community. We are never to nourish grievances, especially within the family. When bitter and hurtful things have been said, we are to do something about it immediately. Apology must be offered for wrongs committed. That way the hurt can be overcome and things won't spiral out of control – as far as the court-room, or even prison. We can't presume that an apology will be accepted, but we can ensure that one is offered.

The world is full of cycles of violence, some of the most bitter being within families. Jesus addresses this endemic human problem head-on. For his followers, the blood-feud, the vendetta, the act motivated by desire for revenge is completely unacceptable. There has to be a better way; and there is.

Thought for the day

We talk of 'cycles of violence'. What about 'cycles of re-conciliation'? How would they start and how could they be built up?

Prayer

Lord, when I give offence please make me a willing to recognise my fault, especially when I have given offence to a member of my family, or a sister or brother in the family of Jesus. May I then, for my part, not only be reconciled, but a reconciler too. Amen

'But I say to you: love your enemies.'

Dt 26:16–19; Ps 119; Mt 5:43–48

> *'You have heard it said; You must love your neighbour*
> *and hate your enemy. But I say to you: love your*
> *enemies and pray for those who persecute you.'*
>
> (Matthew 5:43–44)

The Gospel passage for today marks the culmination of a series of extreme religious teachings: it's not enough to say you mustn't kill – you mustn't even be angry with your brother; it's not enough to say you mustn't commit adultery – you mustn't even have lustful thoughts; it's not enough to say you mustn't swear solemn oaths – you must stick to the plain language of 'Yes' and 'No'. It is not enough to say you must love your neighbour – you must love your enemies and pray for those who persecute you. Jesus sets an extraordinary standard, so far beyond human experience, we might say, as to be practically useless.

And yet, when his enemies finally trap him, this is what he does. As he is crucified, he says, 'Father, forgive them for they do not know what they are doing.' Did he really love the scribes and the Pharisees, the Sadducees and the Romans, who together did away with him? The accounts we have of his death are remarkably detailed, and they all attest that he died without a bitter word for anyone. More than that, he died with a prayer of forgiveness, placing himself in the hands of God; he died

22

knowing his work of reconciliation was complete; he died with the trust of a child peacefully falling asleep.

Thought for the day
'Father forgive them for they do not know what they are doing.' Who are 'they'?

Prayer
Lord, when testing times come, and I am confronted with people who wish to harm both me and those I love, may I find the grace not to hate those people in return, but somehow to see them in the light of your love. Amen

Anthea Dove

Second Week of Lent

Second Sunday of Lent

Leaving home

Gen 12:1–4; Ps 33; 2 Tim 1:8–10

When Abram left his country and everything familiar to him, he made a great leap of faith. He was literally travelling into the unknown with a long and arduous journey ahead of him.

Even today, it is an adventure and a challenge to uproot ourselves from our own country and make a new life for ourselves elsewhere. Of course a lot depends on our motive for emigrating. As a young woman I travelled from England to India without a moment's hesitation because I was going out to be married to the man I loved.

But in recent years people have left their own countries for very different reasons. They flee to escape persecution, torture, rape or murder. Many have the idea that if only they can reach Britain they will be welcome and assured of safety. Sadly they are often disappointed on both counts. They are met with cold officialdom, interrogated in a language they do not understand and lodged in a detention centre or substandard housing while they wait to hear whether or not they will be allowed to stay.

I met a young Indian girl who told us how her family were put in an empty council flat. All the windows were broken; there was no furniture, fridge or cooker. When this young woman went out of the house, the neighbours pelted her with bricks. She said, 'You English people like our curry; why don't you like us?'

The government takes a hard line against asylum seekers, and many of the popular newspapers wage a crusade against them, thus inflaming the hostility which many people feel towards strangers. So it falls to fair-minded, compassionate men and women to befriend people seeking asylum, to go out of their way to listen to their stories of the country they left behind, and to help them in practical ways.

Abram was courageous to leave his country and strike out on a completely new venture, but in the Negeb he was not met by coldness and suspicion.

Thought for the day
Jesus said: 'I was a stranger and you made me welcome.'

Prayer
Lord, help us to get to know the strangers in our midst, to welcome, befriend and learn from them. Give us the sensitivity to stand in their shoes and the compassion to take practical steps on their behalf. Amen

True Christianity

Dan 9:4–10; Ps 79; Lk 6:36–38

> *'Be compassionate as your Father is compassionate.'*
> (Luke 6:36)

Janet made a point of reading the scriptures every day and she was familiar with this text from Luke's gospel. It was one that gave her satisfaction. She thought to herself: 'I reckon I've cracked this one. I am compassionate, I am non-judgemental and forgiving, I give away as much as I can afford.' She had 'ticked all the boxes' and it was a good feeling.

Janet didn't think much of a woman called Dorothy who lived in the same parish. As chair of the Justice and Peace group she had tried several times to persuade Dorothy to come to meetings about burning issues, but in vain. Dorothy was a widow, retired, but she didn't come to weekday Mass, or attend Quiet Days organised by the Sisters of the parish. Janet wondered what she did with her time.

Then, one evening in winter, Janet came across an old man huddled in a doorway. She felt very sorry for him and hurried home to the cupboard where she kept her bed linen. There was one blanket that she particularly liked: it was thick and fleecy. She hesitated, then, wanting to be generous, she pulled that one out of the pile and carried it out into the street. As she came near the place where she had left him, she saw that the old man was now standing up, and someone was holding his arm. She walked up to them.

'Oh, hello, Janet. This is Jack. Jack, this is my friend, Janet,' Dorothy said. 'Jack says he's cold and hungry,' she added, 'so I'm taking him home. A good night's rest will do him good.'

Janet walked home slowly, still carrying the blanket and feeling rather foolish. She realised that she had a lot to learn.

If we are trying to live Christian lives, it's not a good idea to become too preoccupied with our sinfulness or lack of it. Janet was serious and sincere in her efforts to be good, but she didn't have the spontaneous, generous love which motivated Dorothy.

Thought for the day
If we want to be truly Christian, we need to be self-aware.

Prayer
Dear Lord,
teach us to know ourselves
and to be generous and open-hearted in our treatment of others.
Amen

Extravagance?

Is 1:10, 16–20; Ps 51; Mt 23:1–12

> *'Anyone exalts himself will be humbled.'*
>
> (Matthew 23:12)

I read Matthew's words the day after watching the Archbishop of York on television, celebrating in the Minster. When I saw his vestments I laughed with delight, because they were so extravagantly colourful. The difference between this prelate and the Pharisees with their broad headbands and longer tassels, is not so much in their apparel as in their attitudes. There is nothing pompous or attention-seeking about John Sentamu; he is a humble, joyful man of the people who loves to celebrate his faith with music and colour.

I remember once reacting with dismay when a missionary friend of mine told me about a magnificent new church which had been built in a remote part of an African country where the people were desperately poor. It seemed all wrong to me. I pointed out that we can worship God anywhere, the plainest hut or even just a grassy space in the jungle would do. 'Any available money should be spent on the poor, surely?' I asked.

But my friend shook his head. 'The people I work among often go hungry,' he said, 'but they are hungry in other ways, too. They longed to give glory to God and express their adoration for him in their own beautiful new church. The first time they met to worship there, they were ecstatic. You could have heard the drumming and singing miles away.'

I am not convinced. Like most people, I love to wander through our wonderful cathedrals and churches, but I feel just as close to God in a Friends' Meeting House. I admire the gorgeous robes that some of our bishops wear on special occasions, but there is a lot to be said for the Franciscan habit!

Perhaps people like me do well to remember the re-action of Jesus to the woman who broke a jar of costly ointment to anoint his feet. Far from scolding her for her extravagance, he said, 'In truth I tell you, wherever throughout the whole world the gospel is proclaimed, what she has done will be told as well, in remembrance of her' (Matthew 26: 13).

Thought for the day
There is a time for singing and a time for silence.

Prayer
Dear Lord, give us open minds and the ability to see both sides of an argument. Help us to discern where there is need for exuberance, and where there is need for simplicity. Amen

Number One First

Jer 18:18–20; Ps 31; Mt 20:17–28

> *'Promise me that my sons may sit one at your right
> hand and one at your left in your kingdom.'*
> (Matthew 20:21)

I have a lot of sympathy with the mother of James and
John. Although it's a long time ago, I clearly remember
standing at the edge of the field at my son's Sports Day
and shouting myself hoarse as I urged him to win. Most
of us mothers can behave like this. The mother of
Zebedee's sons was bold for a woman of her time, and a
tad over-ambitious, having the temerity to plan the
seating arrangements in heaven, but at least she asked
nothing for herself.

Most of us have a tendency to put Number One, in
other words, Me, first. Often it happens in pretty
insignificant, harmless ways. For instance, if I enter a
room in someone's house on a cold night, I tend to take
the chair nearest the fire. And if there's a single space left
in the car park, I rush to grab it before anyone else sees
it. Isn't it over-scrupulous to be concerned over such
trivialities? Not if they are symptomatic of a general
me-first attitude.

When my bishop, John Crowley, was the bishop for
Cafod, he went with members of the organisation to visit
Africa. It was the time of the horrendous famine in
Southern Ethiopia, and the bishop told me how he had

watched a line of children queuing up to receive their ration of food. It was explained to him that as food was so scarce, only children under four were allowed any. The bishop watched as an older boy carefully and gently fed his little brother, taking not a drop for himself.

It is sobering to compare that young boy's attitude with the prevailing way of looking at things in our society. Recently, I heard a politician say that unless we replace the Trident submarines, we will be in danger of losing our place at the world's top table. Surely Britain has had its turn at the high table, in the days of our Empire? In the world's playground, Britain is not the biggest bully, but sadly, we have joined that bully's gang.

Thought for the day
Number One last: it's demanding, but it's worth trying.

Prayer
Dear Lord,
help us to overcome our egotism,
and teach us to be cheerful in putting the needs of others before our own.
Amen

Simple living

Jer 17:5–10, Ps 1; Lk 16:19–31

Of all the wonderful tales that Jesus tells, the one that makes me most uncomfortable is the story of Dives and Lazarus. It isn't clear whether the rich man knew about the poor man at his gate. Possibly he noticed him and other beggars, but didn't pause to think about their lives.

The trouble is, I do know. I do know that I live and enjoy myself in the affluent part of the world, while thousands of children are dying of starvation in developing countries. When I buy a new dress, I know that my sisters in refugee camps have only rags to wear. Today when I take care to eat five fruits and vegetables to keep me healthy, I know that countless people will be eating nothing at all.

Last week some good Christian friends invited me to dinner. They gave me champagne, smoked salmon, avocado, cambozola cheese to mention only some of the delicious fare. As we ate we started talking about the terrible state of the world and its dreadful inequalities. But talking is not enough. I am very far from living simply so that others may simply live.

Of all my friends, only one, whom I will call Isla, truly lives a simple life. She lives in an old gypsy caravan which has no heating, on land belonging to a farmer who charges no rent in return for her work as his shepherd. Isla earns a little money from looking after other people's dogs, or houses, or children, and just now she has a temporary job for which she is paid a small salary, growing organic vegetables and looking after groups of young offenders in a remote and beautiful part of Scotland. She eats the simplest food and doesn't buy clothes, wearing what people give her. Although in her young life Isla has suffered grievously, she always seems happy. She is only half my age, but I look up to her. I think that if I could live more like Isla, I would be living more as God wants me to live.

Thought for the day
How happy are the poor in spirit; theirs is the Kingdom of heaven.

Prayer
Lord, teach us not to be overly concerned with our material welfare, but instead to find our treasure in the coming of the Kingdom. Amen

Courage

Gen 37:34, 12–13, 17–28; Ps 05; Mt 21:33–43, 45–46

The story of Joseph and his coat of many colours has probably captured the imagination of readers since it was first written thousands of years ago. It is a kind of adventure story, with plenty of drama. Joseph is innocent and good, his brothers crafty and wicked. But there are exceptions, two brothers who dare to speak out against the majority. It is doubtful whether Judah's intervention was pure in its intention, for he had an eye to the main chance: he saw an opportunity to make money. But he did point out that Joseph was 'our brother and our flesh', words which may have been sincerely meant.

Reuben, however, was genuinely dismayed at his brothers' plot. He dared to speak his mind, because he was anxious to save young Joseph. It always takes courage to be the one who makes an unpopular suggestion in the face of united hostility.

Danny lived with his alcoholic mother on a run-down estate. He was thrilled when Big Mac invited him to join his gang. Danny was the youngest member at twelve. In the evenings, his mother was either at the pub or asleep, so it was easy for Danny to slip out and join the others. At first he loved the excitement, but when Big Mac told him to get a knife he hesitated. 'Scared?' Mac asked, and a few of the other guys laughed. Next day, Danny got his knife. He had never stolen anything before, but he wasn't caught. He felt proud.

The following night, Danny sensed that something big was about to happen.

'We're going to get Lennie Potts,' said Tone, Mac's mate. 'He's a grass and he's asking for it.' He whipped out his knife and showed Danny the sharp blade. 'Got your knife, kid? Look, Lennie's coming this way. He won't know what's hit him!' Tone's jeering laugh horrified Danny. 'No!' he said, then he shouted, 'Lennie, run!' It was Danny who ended up in hospital with nine stab wounds.

Thought for the day

In the gospels, Jesus says over and over again to his disciples: 'Do not be afraid', yet we continue to be frightened, timid, lacking courage.

Prayer

Lord, give us the courage to do what is right, even when it costs us dearly. Help us to be unafraid of criticism and challenge. We pray for the children who live in poverty, and for those who have to grow up unloved. Help us not to be lazy or apathetic about involvement in issues of justice. Amen

Second Saturday of Lent

Great love

Mic 7:14–15; Ps 103:1–4, 9–12; Lk 15:1–3, 11–32

If there was a prize for the greatest story ever told, Christ's story of the Prodigal Son would surely win it. Except for the fact that no women are mentioned, it has all the ingredients of a good yarn: interesting characters, plenty of drama and suspense. But of course it is none of these things that make it so memorable; the really remarkable thing about this story is the way it reveals to us the love-without-limit that God has for each one of us.

He will forgive us, accept us, and love us whatever we do, whatever sort of people we are. That is why this story, from the lips of Jesus, is so powerful.

And, of course, there is a corollary. We can't be deeply thankful for this unconditional love from God without at least trying to offer the same total acceptance to others. I wish I had the great-hearted extravagant love for my brothers and sisters that the father in the story has for the younger son. But I'm afraid that I, and I guess most of us, have more in common with the older son. We can be petty-minded, sulky, jealous and envious.

But some exceptional people do come close to loving in the way that God loves. One of my friends, whom I will call Mary, has a daughter, Susie. At fourteen, she was a bright and happy girl, but six months later she was hooked on drugs. She stole from her mother, first money, then jewellery.

Mary tried everything. She organised counselling for

Susie but she failed to turn up for the appointments. She persuaded her to go to a rehabilitation centre; she ran away. Then she left home, and six months later Mary went to visit her in an institution for young offenders. At twenty-five Susie had been in prison three times; at twenty-six she disappeared.

For six years Mary had no news of her. 'It's time to let go, Mary,' a friend gently advised her. Mary shook her head. 'I'll never let go,' she said. 'I love her.'

Thought for the day
Greater love hath no man than the father of the Prodigal Son.

Prayer
Dear Lord, we thank you with full hearts for loving us unconditionally.
Teach us to deepen our love for you and for all the people in our lives.
Amen

Robert Kaggwa

Third week of Lent

Third Sunday of Lent

An unexpected encounter

Ex 17:3–7; Ps 95; Rom 5:1–2, 5–8; Jn 4:5–42

> *'Many Samaritans of that town believed in him on the strength of the woman's testimony.'* (John 4:39)

This is a Sunday of surprises. Apart from reminding us of the love of God poured into our hearts, we are invited to open up to the power of the Spirit, the God of surprises who is often symbolised by living water. Are our lives determined by the past or the future? Most of us are trained to think we are the sum of our past experiences and traditions. That is why it is often difficult to change. That is why we often fail to let go, to turn towards the future and believe in God's future.

In his book, *With Open Hands*, Henri Nouwen told a story of a woman who was brought to a psychiatric centre. She was wild, swinging at everything in sight, and scaring everyone so much that the doctors had to take everything away from her. But there was a small coin which she gripped in her fist. It took two nurses to pry open her hand. It was as though she would lose her very self along with the coin. If they deprived her of that last possession, she would have nothing more and be nothing more. This is what she feared.

But the woman in the gospel lets go. She is freed from her fears through the encounter with this one man for whom the traditions and boundaries erected by humans do not count. She will in turn be Jesus' messenger to her own world that has created discriminations that she is victim of.

To convert means to let go of the past, to let go of our fears and to believe in God's future, which is full of new possibilities. We are asked to let this new, unheard-of-message change our lives, to let ourselves be overtaken by this great news and to look at reality in a new way.

Thought for the day

What is that I am holding on to? What is preventing me seeing the God of surprises acting in this world?

Prayer

Loving and gracious God, you never cease to surprise us. When we are weary you show us that we are totally cared for.
When we get so attached to our traditions you move us to see the larger picture.
Let us let go of the past and trust in your future of justice and peace.
Amen

A truth larger than ourselves

2 Kings 5:1–15; Ps 42–43; Lk 4:24–30

> *Like Elijah and Elisha Jesus is not sent to the Jews only.*

Someone died and went to heaven. There she fell into a big party. Everyone was rejoicing. It was like a big village party. People were dancing, eating and drinking. Muslims, Hindus, Jews, Christians, Sikhs and many others were partying. The person walked around to see what was happening in other parts of heaven. As she walked around she saw a group of people in a tent celebrating alone. She asked Jesus who those people were. Jesus replied, 'Don't worry about them. Those are the self-righteous believers. They think they are the only ones here.'

Our world is divided by all sorts of conflict – religious, political, economic, and ethnic. The cause of Christianity is not helped by claiming that that no real good can be found in other faiths or cultures. We can be proud of our own community without despising those who are not 'one of us'. Elijah was sent not to his people but to the poor widow from Sidon, and so was Elisha sent to the Syrian leper. Jesus too was not sent just to his own people but to all, and he exemplified this in his actions and teachings. Jesus insists on inclusiveness. That is his vision. That is what he lived and died for. He calls on each of us to be tolerant and inclusive people.

Christian tolerance is not weakness or a lazy acceptance of whatever movement happens to be in vogue. Christian tolerance is a reverence for the truth that is always larger than ourselves; it is recognition of the charity that flourishes beyond the reaches of our borders; it is a profound respect for the freedom of God to move in his chosen way. It is a humility before the greatness of God.

Thought for the day
If God risks hoping in us, why should we deny his hope in others?

Prayer
All loving and inclusive God,
your message of love and compassion was long proclaimed by your prophets
Send women and men to proclaim this again today.
Make us all instruments of reconciliation!
Amen

Third Tuesday of Lent

When night ends and the day begins

Dn 3:25, 34–43; Ps 25; Mt 18:21–35

May the contrite soul, the humbled spirit be acceptable to you.

The word 'obedience' means 'to listen deeply'. This is the beginning of humility. We know that to listen deeply requires the loss of ourselves, to forget ourselves. It means allowing the voice of the other to be heard. Jesus listened deeply to God within his heart and he was able to accept what God had asked of him, to allow himself to be lifted up so that he could draw all things to himself.

Jesus' message is that God has fallen in love with humanity! The totally new reality that has broken into the world with Jesus of Nazareth is the revelation of God's forgiving, inclusive, unconditional acceptance of all men and women. It is also the revelation of what it is to be truly human in a world that is often dehumanised.

We cannot forgive if we do not become humble. We must forgive not only seven times but seventy seven times. Our forgiveness should reach no boundaries. Forgiveness is for giving. We should give it to all without reserve. To be humble is to become obedient and recognise everyone as intrinsically good, a sister, a brother and a friend.

An old Rabbi once asked his disciples how they could tell when the night ended and the day began. The disciples scratched their heads. 'Could it be,' asked one, 'when you see an animal in the distance and know whether it's a sheep or a dog?' 'No,' replied the Rabbi. 'Could it be,' another asked, 'when you see a tree in the distance and can tell whether it is a fig tree or a peach tree?' 'No,' said the Rabbi.

'Well then, when is it?' his pupils demanded. 'It is when you can look at the face of any man or woman and see that he is your brother or she is your sister. Because if you cannot do this, then no matter what time it is, it is still night.'

Thought for the day
Forgiveness and humility go hand in hand.

Prayer
Loving and generous God, you never cease to forgive.
Jesus taught us that it is only in forgiving that we are pardoned.
Make us humble.
And give us a thirst for justice in this torn world.
Amen

'Good guys' and 'bad guys'

Dt 4:1, 5–9; Ps 147; Mt 5:17–19

Take notice of the laws and observe them.

Without law any community loses its structure and easily succumbs to anarchy and destruction. Jesus said, 'I have not come to abolish the Law but to complete it' (Matthew 5: 17). This will be fulfilled in his teaching about the law of love that perfects all laws and teachings.

The contradiction of seeing celebrations of war and celebrations of love at the same time is a sign of the terrible mess our world is in. We pick and choose from the laws that God has given us. We are deeply divided and the rhetoric of hatred is gaining centre stage. We celebrate the global village and rejoice in people coming closer together thanks to modern means of communication. But while human beings have never been so close together, yet they have never been so deeply divided. Our leaders say that the world is in deep trouble because of other people, because of the 'axis of evil'. This is the frightening politics of dividing the world into 'good guys' and 'bad guys'.

But are we not all a mixed bag? To label people as either the 'good guys' or the 'bad guys' is childish. Our world is badly in need of healing. If we demonise others, we dehumanise this beautiful, complex world that God has created. Wherever we do this, whether in society, in our workplace, in our schools, communities or families, we only make others and ourselves suffer. The politics of 'good guys' and 'bad guys' is the source of war, and of violence and division in society and in families. True reconciliation cannot come with this type of politics. It is the politics of the night.

Thought for the day
True reconciliation is only possible through the law of love.

Prayer
God of love, teach the true meaning of law. Open our eyes to new possibilities of your love and forgiveness in this divided world. Amen

Listening to God's voice

Jr 7:23–28; Ps 95; Lk 11:14–23

> *'Oh that today you would listen to his voice! Harden not your heart!'* (Psalm 95)

Today's readings invite us to listen to God's voice. This is the teaching of the prophet Jeremiah in the first reading. It is also Jesus' teaching in today's gospel reading. Listening is not an easy thing. As the saying goes, 'People only hear what they want to hear'. The Psalmist too calls on people not to harden their hearts but to listen to God's voice.

Jesus' teaching received mixed reactions. His radical message was often disturbing. 'He who is not with me is against me.' Some were attentive to his word but many thought that he was possessed by demons. If people thought that he cast demons in the name of the King of devils, then that was a sure sign that they had got it wrong. They had not listened to him. They were unable to distinguish between good and evil.

We live in confusing times. We have to face the reality of our weakness and vulnerability. We often get it wrong. We must open our ears. Only listening to God's word leads to true discernment.

We all need a power that can sustain us through our difficulties. This is even more important today – when there are so many conflicts, so much war and terrorism. To believe in the abiding presence of a God who cares for us gives us a deep sense of joy in the midst of our stops and starts. It is a presence that always challenges our generosity and calls on our sense of justice. It keeps us on our toes. It will sustain us even when bad news continues to be a regular feature on our televisions.

The time of Lent, as we walk towards Easter, is a time to examine the quality of our listening.

Thought for the day
Harden not your heart.

Prayer
Loving and caring God, send us your Spirit to loosen our hearts so that we can listen to your word and discern what is good from what is evil. Amen

Third Friday of Lent

Images of God

Hos 14:2–10; Ps 81, Mk 12:8–34

> *'We will not say anymore "Our God" to what our own hands have made.'* (Hosea 14:4)

We all have images of God in our minds – some are good and others are bad. The prophet Hosea calls on the people not to have false images of God or idols. Jesus also wants to transform our images of God. In each of us there is an image or picture of reality, whether conscious or not, which more than anything else shapes the way we live. Jesus takes his listeners back to Israel's creed: 'Listen Israel, the Lord our God is the one Lord, you must love the Lord with all your heart, with all your soul, with all your mind and with all your strength' (Mark 12: 29–30).

The false images that we may have about God can be sad and damaging. These images can originate in early childhood and are not easily wiped out. It's not only the contemporaries of Jesus who had this problem. We may also worship false gods. For example, the vengeful or punitive God-Who-Didn't-Give-Me-What-I-Asked-For, the God who fails to live up to our expectations or to co-operate with our plans. This is the God who has been called the 'manipulated God'. We often hear the complaint, 'What good is a God who never answers my prayers?' It is so difficult for us to understand that God will not be manipulated, neither by prayers nor by good works.

48

The most damaging image of all is a God who is angry, out to 'get me', always looking around for wrongdoers. This is a God who needs to be appeased. When thinking of this God you feel guilty and worthless. This is not the kind of God that Jesus reveals to us. This is not the God of Jesus Christ.

In his actions and in his parables Jesus gives us the true image of God. This is the God of life, compassion, the God of forgiveness, the God of unconditional love. And Jesus shows that believing in this true image of God means loving our neighbour as well. Both go hand in hand. There is no commandment greater than that.

Thought for the day
You must love the Lord with all your heart and you must love your neighbour as yourself.

Prayer
Loving and gracious God renew us by Jesus' teaching to see you clearly as the God who loves and renews us each day. Amen

Love not sacrifice

Hos 5:15–6: 6; Ps 51; Lk 18:9–14

> *'What I want is love not sacrifice; knowledge of God,*
> *not holocausts.'* (Hosea 6:6)

This message of Hosea is echoed in the gospel parable of the Pharisee and the publican. The parables were not harmless stories that Jesus narrated to his contemporaries but they were subversive. In the gospel story it is the despised tax collector, not the religious leader and teacher, the Pharisee, who goes home at rights with God.

The parables are still subversive today. In a world in which sinners stood ineluctably excluded and condemned, Jesus' acceptance and openness to them was irresistible. Contact with him triggered repentance. After communion with him, conversion followed. By eating and drinking with people often marginalized or condemned, Jesus was enacting in deed what he had already announced in word: the breaking in of the gratuitous love of God's Reign in the *now* of their existence. Nothing could have dramatised the gratuity and the present-realization of God's saving love more effectively than this unheard-of initiative of inviting outcasts and sinners to join him as he ate and drank. It was sheer gift, a radically new relationship of grace.

When the Pharisees and teachers saw Jesus eating and drinking with tax collectors and other outcasts of society, they criticized Jesus. 'Why do you eat and drink with tax collectors and sinners?' they demanded. In the context of first century Palestine, Jesus' behaviour was a strikingly original characteristic of his ministry and an indication of how he understood his own identity and mission. A totally new reality had broken in; a new way of relating was being set up, a new way of being together was being demonstrated; in a word – a new way of being human was being revealed in the lifestyle of Jesus of Nazareth.

So, the Publican, not the respectable religious teacher, goes home justified and this is entirely in the logic of Jesus' ministry.

Thought for the day
Compassion not pious talk; love not sacrifice.

Prayer
Loving and merciful God, open our hearts to your compassion. May we be compassionate as you are compassionate. Amen

Hugo Slim

Fourth Week of Lent

Fourth Sunday of Lent

Seeing new things

Jn 9:1–41

> *'Surely we are not blind, are we?'* (John 9:40)

What a wonderful thing that a person who has been blind from birth and never seen the world should be healed in a moment. What an infuriating thing that, instead of celebrating such a miracle, almost everybody around him soon gets caught up in a dispute about it. Was it a trick? If this was a good deed, was it done by a wicked man? Whose fault was it that he was born blind in the first place?

Human beings are cautious. We can be resistant to new things, especially things which claim to be good news. We are often more comfortable with bad news or with ways of thinking which mean we need not expect too much from our lives. Life is hard. We plod along. It could be worse. When God reaches out and touches us or the world around us we may prefer to dispute it than celebrate it.

Today's new wave of conviction atheists think that God is something to argue about. But he is not. God is something to be felt and known. Like the healed man, we can know God most easily when we realize that he cares for us and loves us. This experience of God may come through other people, or directly in a sense of faith. Only the man who had felt God in this story had no problem with what happened. It was obvious to him. There was no need to suspect anyone, to find fault with anyone or to argue with anyone. What happened was simply God.

God's actions often challenge us to see something new happening in our lives. God works most with newness. Acknowledging new things can be particularly difficult for people who think they know everything already. Better than an expert faith is an open and curious faith which constantly reminds us that we do not know every-thing and that what we do know can sometimes stop us from seeing new things.

Thought for the day
A gifted amateur may see God at work more clearly than a religious expert.

Prayer
Lord, open my eyes to what you do around me.
Keep my soul curious and my faith alert to what you actually do
instead of what I expect you to do. Amen

The Words of God

Jn 4:43–54

> *The man believed the word that Jesus spoke to him and started on his way.* (John 4:50)

I am writing this near St Peter's cathedral in Geneva, where the reformer John Calvin spent thousands of hours preaching in the sixteenth century. My family is in the middle of moving house from Geneva to Oxford. We are surrounded by packing cases and I only have a copy of the New Testament to hand, which explains why all my reflections are from John's gospel.

Calvin believed that we can be changed by hearing the word of God. It works upon us. It can reach deep into our being. For Calvin, the word of God in Scripture was the ultimate sacrament. And we receive this sacrament by believing what we hear. This act of believing is deeper than just hearing. It is a kind of spiritual concentration and reorientation in which we accept God's word and understand it for ourselves so that it changes the way we are and the way we act.

Jesus initially misjudges the royal official from Capernaum. He thinks he is yet another person who needs signs and wonders to believe. But he is not. He has faith. He is open to God and ready for what God will say. God's word is enough. The anguished official believes that Jesus' short sentence will change the world. The words move him immediately and he starts to walk for home.

Jewish people talk of the scriptures as being sweet like honey – and something that can make us sweeter too. Words and language are a mysterious part of human beings but they are powerful and not a little divine. Christ comes very close to us in scripture in the text upon the page or the word from the pulpit. God is incarnate and effective in these words. He needs few words to change us – 'Go; your son will live.'

Thought for the day
Choosing four or five words of God each morning, and tasting them, is a good way to stay close to God and let him change us.

Prayer
Lord, let me taste your words – a sacrament to nourish and transform me. Amen

Letting Others Act

Jn 5:1–3, 5–16.

'Do you want to be made well?' (John 5:6)

It is often hard for children to understand why they have to learn grammar. 'If I can speak in French,' pleads my daughter, 'what does it matter if I know whether or not I am using the imperfect or the perfect tense?' The answer, perhaps, is that grammar is more a training for life than for speech, because there is a grammar to our lives and to the politics around us.

Unless we understand the grammar of Jesus' healing miracle by the pool at Bethsaida we will not understand who worked the miracle. Jesus asks the paralysed man if he would like 'to be made well'. In other words, he asks if he would like to be healed passively – to have something done to him. The man explains that he can never get to the water in time because there is no one to do it for him. Jesus does not do it for him either but simply tells him to move from a passive frame of mind to an active one - do it yourself. He does, and heals himself.

The grammar of politics is important too, particularly when our politics is concerned with helping others who are poor or faced with war or disaster. It is tempting for us to make the poor the object of our politics. 'We' help 'Them'. But this is not good politics. People who are affected by injustice need to be active in the struggle for justice. Freedom is best won by those who need and want it. Like the man at Bethsaida, people have to make movements of their own and not wait for movements across distant waters. Aid which keeps people sitting down is not good aid. Words which encourage them to stand up are better.

Thought for the day
Consider the grammar in any personal or political encounter.

Prayer
Lord, help me to judge the grammar
of my relationships with others.
Advise me when I am best an active verb
or am more useful as a preposition
to work *with* people or *beside* them.
And then tell me when I would best be still
as the object of their giving.

Fourth Wednesday of Lent

Watching God in Christ

Jn 5:17–30

> *'Truly, I tell you, the Son can do nothing on his own,*
> *but only what he sees the Father doing.'* (John 5:19)

This is one of several passages in John's Gospel in which Jesus talks theology and sets about explaining the relationship between himself and God. These can be quite complicated, even convoluted, sections which explain the mechanics of the Father–Son relationship and, later on, the Trinitarian relationship between Father, Son and Holy Spirit. When I was studying theology at university, I had a friend who did brilliant and irreverent imitations of these passages which invariably ended up by thoroughly confusing and amusing us all. He has since become a successful banker.

Although John's descriptions of Jesus' relationship with God can sometimes sound mechanical, they are really deeply mystical. In this one, Jesus tells us that he is a reflection of God - so much a part of God that he moves as one with God and does whatever he sees God doing. This is the great blessing of the incarnation - that in Christ's words, life, death and resurrection we can come to know what God is like. In Christ we can watch God. And, as we watch him, we can come to know him and be changed and comforted by him. We can even become a little like him too.

When Moses collected the law, he looked upon God

and his face shone so much that he had to wear a veil so as not to dazzle the Israelites on his return. Christians believe that Christ is actually of God so that in him we see what God is doing. Christ's life, death and resurrection unveil God for us. This conviction is the basis of John's exceptional insight into the incarnation which he famously summarizes in the Prologue of his gospel: 'Noone has ever seen God. It is God the only Son, who is close to the Father's heart, who has made him known.' This revelation is Christ's gift to us.

Thought for the day
In Jesus we can see what God is like.

Prayer
Lord Jesus Christ,
as you watch the Father, may I watch you.
And, as I watch you, be changed by what you see. Amen

St John's Mistake

Jn 5:31–47

> *'But I know that you do not have the love of God in you.'* (John 5:42)

A terrible struggle between God and religion, love and law, charisma and bureaucracy, risks and rules, prophecy and order, grace and violence runs throughout John's Gospel These conflicts lie at the heart of our human condition. In John they come together as a deeper clash between light and darkness. Jesus is the 'true light' while the powers of this world are the darkness.

Reading John's gospel made me a Christian when I was a teenager. Christ was incredibly powerful, easily won every argument and knew exactly what – as God – he was doing here on earth. By contrast, the religious and political world around him was stupid, hypocritical and blind. This is just how many teenagers feel about the world and I was glad that God did too. But as I got older, I grew impatient with the black and white certainties of John's Gospel. The worldly powers are sometimes embodied in a group John calls 'the Jews'. Obviously, this group did not include all Jews because Jesus himself was Jewish and many other Jewish people listened to Jesus, were healed by him, followed him, became his disciples and loved him. The people who John lumps together as 'the Jews' were the rigorously religious authorities who challenged Jesus, could not recognize him as God's Son and eventually may have contributed to his execution. John has Jesus judge this group harshly. To say that you do not have the love of God in you is one of the hardest things you can say to a religious person.

John's labelling of a clique of religious authorities as 'the Jews' has contributed to the tragedy of almost two thousand years of anti-semitism. Jesus did not object to Jewish people but to a universal human trait which can fail to recognize God and which prioritizes its own dogma and institutions over love and compassion. John wanted to draw clear lines between light and darkness. But his label stigmatized Jesus' own people, a people beloved by Jesus and by God.

Thought for the day
When we hate whole groups and stop seeing the God-made individuals within them, we do not have the love of God in us.

Prayer
Lord Jesus, you had enemies and told us we would too. Hold me back from making enemies too easily and from feeling I need enemies to prove that I am right. Amen

More shepherds, fewer fences

Jn 7:1–2; 10:25–30.

> *'You do not belong to my sheep. My sheep hear my
> voice. I know them and they follow me.'*

(John 10:26–27)

After a damning statement, here is a divisive one. John
likes a spiritual world in which borders are clearly
marked and fences well maintained, a world in which
people's position as pro-Christ or anti-Christ is obvious.
But should we be the same? Can sheep only have one
shepherd? Does God only have one flock?

Not long after the Al Qaeda attacks on New York and
Washington, my personal life was breaking apart. On
one particularly painful day, I fell in step with a Muslim
cleric as we walked to the same railway station in
Swansea and then boarded the same train. He could tell
that I was suffering and for an hour and a half he listened
to me, comforted me and taught me some important
insights from Islam before getting off the train a few
stops before me. It was one of the most loving pastoral
encounters I have ever had and certainly well timed. God
was in his words and in his kindness.

CAFOD and Christian Aid work through and for
people who are not Christians and never will be. The
work of these agencies embodies the love of God and
shares his purpose for people everywhere. God works
through many different shepherds and has many dif-

ferent flocks. If we offer ourselves and our Christian organizations as shepherds for others then we should not be surprised if we also experience God's shepherding through people from other faiths or none. It is not which group or flock we are in that counts for God but the relationships we are in – with God, with each other and with ourselves. Christ called us to be open to God so that we can hear his voice and follow him. What broke his heart was when people refused to believe that, like a shepherd, God is continuously guarding, guiding and calling all of us to a life of love and forgiveness.

We can put such high fences around us that we cannot hear God in those outside. Instead, we only hear our own voices echoing off our well-made walls – echoes we then frequently mistake for the voice of God himself.

Thought for the day
We all belong to God who calls and cares for us all.

Prayer
Lord God, continue to call me wherever I am
Through whomever I am with
So I may never go too far from you. Amen

The benefit of doubt

Jn 7:40–52

> *'Why did you not arrest him?'* (John 7:45)

The police often (but not always!) find themselves caught in the middle of somebody else's fight or picking up the pieces of a conflict not of their own making. Here they are caught between their own intuition and the authority of the Chief Priests.

Jesus has impressed the police as someone other than a blasphemer and they have given him the benefit of the doubt. This doubt stands in stark contrast to the certainty of the chief priests who have been shocked and offended by Jesus and his claims. The police have not been so much offended as amazed. They have held back from a decisive judgement. Jesus has wobbled them.

Many feel that doubt is as important as faith, at least, that it is an important part of keeping a fresh and true faith. At its best, doubt is a kind of creative shudder – more a feeling of intuition than a sense of fact. Doubting is when we begin to think that 'something is not quite right'. It is a healthy instinct we should cherish. Doubt can set us thinking laterally and open up new possibilities. In thrillers, the moment doubt creeps into the mind of a detective is usually the moment when she or he begins to unravel the case, seeing through the false versions of events. Her doubts allow her to discover the truth.

By giving Jesus the benefit of the doubt, the police brought themselves into conflict with their superiors. To act on one's doubts takes courage. At dinner the other night, someone asked me to explain my belief in God. As usual, I failed. Yet I continued to doubt her more articulate account of a Godless world. Like the Temple Police, I am impressed and amazed by Christ. My experience of his life, death and resurrection leave me doubting any account which sees Jesus simply as an ordinary prophet from an unexpected town. I have a sense that this is not quite right. And these doubts mean that I must keep looking into John's extraordinary belief that Jesus is God incarnate and can make God known.

Thought for the day
Doubt is a good friend to an open faith.

Prayer
Lord, bless me with doubt when I need it.
Give me the grace of a holy intuition and a curious faith
Which finds you where others will not look. Amen

Mary Grey
Fifth Week of Lent

Fifth Sunday of Lent

Bringing life out of death

Ezk 37:12–14; Ps 130; Rom 8:8–11; Jn 11:1–45

It was a bright, sunny morning in Kigali, the mountain-ringed capital of Rwanda, land of a thousand hills. It was 10 years on after the genocide, yet for the people who told their stories that day, the tragic events could have happened last week. It was the words of André Kara-maga, a Presbyterian minister who had suffered many personal losses, that pierced me most deeply. 'My image of our Church here now is of Ezechiel's dried bones: the tragic slaughter in my country has robbed us of life.'

How to restore life? is today's theme, and it will become increasingly highlighted as we move closer to the death and Resurrection of Jesus. The Martha of John's Gospel today is not the Martha of Luke's Gospel, much troubled about domestic affairs. She is the householder and probably a leader in her community. It is the quality of her faith in Jesus as the Son of God that evokes his revelation to her that he is 'the Resurrection' and that to whoever believe in him will live forever. Let us not miss the significance of this: in the synoptic Gospels it is Peter who confesses faith in Jesus as the Son of God. Here, Resurrection faith is on the lips of Martha, a woman, whose role has often been forgotten.

If it were not for Martha's confession, we might be tempted to think that the whole point of the story is the raising to life of Lazarus. But Lazarus would still die in the future, as we all will. The point of faith in the Risen Christ is to believe and to hope that however traumatic the reality, the wounded memories of slaughter, the violence of war and rape or the misery of watching children dying of famine, that this is not the last word: God longs for life in its fullness and justice for all. Whether it be Rwanda, Darfur or Iraq, Martha's confession of faith and Lazarus's raising are powerful symbols that the lifeless bones of oppression may give way to life-giving possibilities of justice.

Thought for the day
No situation is beyond God's mercy and redemption.

Prayer
Into our confusion, our falling -apart and loss of hope, you offer the memory of Martha who stood firm in Resurrection faith, and the message of Jesus that authentic life is intertwined inseparably with believing in him. Empower our lives with this truth today and always, as we move in faith towards sharing in the mystery of his Resurrection. Amen

Giving voice to the voiceless

Dan 13:1–9, 15–17, 19–30; Ps 23, Jn 8

It is early evening. The thoughts of our group of travellers visiting Wells for India's water projects in the desert of Rajasthan (see www.wellsforindia.org) were turning longingly to supper. But it was not to be. A group of women and children awaited us at the Field Centre with an urgent request. These women were local prostitutes. There was a look of desperation in their faces. Longstanding cycles of poverty had driven them to prostitution. They lived in small, desolate hamlets along the highway where truck drivers travelled the long distances between Delhi and Mumbai, and they saw no hope of escape for themselves. But they were united in seeking a better future for their children. And so Project Asha ('Hope') was born, where Wells for India tried for ten years to educate these children for a different future. In the end, we failed, so enormous were the forces and vested interests ranged against us.

In the story of Susannah, and John's story of the woman caught in the act of adultery, we meet again women struggling with some act of sexual violation. Both stories point to the tragic injustices today of the violation of female sexuality, and the growing trade in child trafficking. In both of our stories today, the women are rescued by others, by Daniel's wisdom in Susannah's case, and by that Jesus in the other.

Why are we given these stories in the build-up to Holy

Week? Is it because Jesus came to reverse a world order based on domination – whether of women and vulnerable children, of colonised and enslaved peoples, of destroyed rain forests and extinct forms of life? This new world order will be one where humiliated women and shamed children would acquire a voice: their own voices will protest, their strengthened spirits will resist, and their hopes of goodness, kindness and dignity will be realised, in the land of the living.

Thought for the day
If victims acquire a voice, who will listen?

Prayer
What did you see, Jesus, when they brought the shamed woman to you? With your heart of compassion did you know what little choice she had? With your mind of judgment did you condemn the hypocrisy that condemned only the woman? Did you walk the thorny path to Calvary raging for what women would undergo through the long travail of history? May your blessed rage for justice be a liberating strength now, today, for women and children, before their lives are destroyed. Amen

The real source of power and life

Num 21:4–9; Ps 102; Jn 8: 21–30

Why do we humans get it so badly wrong? We turn potentially positive gifts of creation into idols, whether it be money (ourselves), golden calves (the Israelites and ourselves), national symbols like the Nazi swastika (all nations trying to dominate others), and absolute power (all tyrants throughout history). We never seem to grasp the fundamental ambiguity of symbols, the way they can be life-giving or death-dealing. None of us can survive without water, the most powerful means of life, literally and symbolically, yet, through global warming and climate change we have recently witnessed the most destructive tidal wave (tsunami) bringing tragedy to thousands of people in Sri Lanka and Indonesia – some of the poorest communities in the world. Oil, a biblical symbol of wealth and of the anointing of kings, prophets and priests, has become a commodity we go to war for. Serpents, too, are no less ambiguous, symbols of both wisdom and cunning. Traditionally, Eve is depicted in the garden of Eden as talking with the serpent and being led astray, with disastrous consequences. Yet the serpent is revered as goddess of wisdom in many near-eastern and Mediterranean civilisations. The Israelites of today's story also experienced this duality: both punished with the serpent's deadly bite, yet healed through God's mercy when they gazed at the bronze serpent lifted high.

Jesus knew this story very well. It was a bitter moment

– one of the many when he tried to explain his actions to an uncomprehending crowd. Just as the Jews were healed when they looked up at the bronze serpent, healing would be offered by his own lifting up, on the Cross. But we still fail to get it. We still idolise the Cross and not its true meaning. We glorify suffering, pain, sacrifice and death for their own sakes, crucifying poor communities and marginalized groups on the cross of the world. What Jesus tells us repeatedly is that he came to bring fullness of life for all, not death. He came to end the necessity of crucifixions, not to ideologise them. His Cross is about the promise of life, risen life with him. That is the true source of power.

Thought for the day
The Cross did not become the central symbol of Christianity until the Emperor Constantine conquered the Roman world, using the Cross as a military symbol of battle.

Prayer
Christ, anointed as prophet by the action of an unnamed woman, forgive us our lack of understanding as to the promise of the symbols of life. Wash away the confusions of our minds and hearts: teach us the true meaning of being 'lifted up'– being lifted up into sharing the fullness of life with you. May we freely commit ourselves to your passion for life and accept the consequences this brings. Amen

The truth will set you free

Dan 3:14–20, 24–28, 52–56; Jn 8:31–42

The God of Israel miraculously preserved the three young men from the fiery furnace of the tyrant – a well-loved story. Yet God did not intervene to save the Beloved Son from a humiliating death. Standing up for the truth, whatever the cost, is the message here – as Jesus' controversy with the Jews makes clear.

Integrity – in public as well as in private – is what is at stake. There have been martyrs throughout history standing up for God's truth and paying the price for it. It is no less a challenge today, when 'masters of spin' govern public life; when even now, it is not publicly declared that there were no 'weapons of mass destruction' – the justification given for war on Iraq. Truth and integrity have been compromised too in Church life, through clergy sexual abuse scandals and the lack of transparency in the way they have been handled.

But what kind of freedom does standing up for truth bring? For Notre Dame Sister Dorothy Stang, standing up against the loggers in the Brazilian rain forest, it brought a violent death, as it did for the courageous journalist Daniel Pearl, as well as for Margaret Hassan, Director of Care International, who refused to abandon the Iraqi children dependent on her. Three contemporary victims of the fiery furnace.

'God is truth' and 'Truth is God' Gandhi said, addressing a group of atheists. But unless as a society we commit ourselves to be pilgrims of the truth, the fiery furnace will continue to claim countless victims.

Thought for the day
If we could only learn to speak the truth of our communal lives, it would change the world

Prayer
God of integrity, may we dream of a common language based on a truth, forged in the depth of hearts burning for justice. May this dream be nourished by a deep listening to the truths of the lives of vulnerable people the world over. May your Spirit of truth gift us with the steadfastness needed to bring to birth these dreams of peace and justice as living reality. Amen

God's covenant with the entire earth

Gen 17:3–9; Ps 105; Jn 8:51–59

'I, the Lord of wind and sky,' so the hymn goes. 'I the Lord who calms wind and waves', the Gospel tells us. And Abraham is called, renamed, and promised the land of Canaan, if he and his descendants keep the covenant. This is the bedrock of Jewish faith, as well as the bedrock of faith in Christ and the New Covenant.

Today we revisit the theme of Covenant with two new contexts: firstly, the consciousness that the Bible Lands are claimed not just by one but by two peoples; secondly, that God's covenant comprehends not only humans, but the entire web of life, all organism, trees, plants and animals. Peace among nations, including the nations of the Holy Land, is intertwined with peace and reconciliation with the earth. The covenant is cosmic.

What struck me most of all recently, on a visit to Palestine/Israel, on leaving the airport, were the barren, rocky hills, with forlorn-looking olive trees on the terraces. Land that had been worked for 10,000 years now rendered un-fertile, un-workable, because the people who carefully tended the terraces had been evicted. And the olive tree is as much loved in Palestine as is the neem tree in India, celebrated in myth and poetry. Commitment to the land, the beloved ha'arets of Israel, has not been extended to both peoples of the land.

Yet within the Jewish and Christian heritage there is a vision of sharing the land between people, trees, and animals. The famous paintings by the American folk artist Edward Hicks of 'The Peaceable Kingdom' depict the scene in the opening verses of Isaiah chapter 11. The wolf lies down with the lamb, and the leopard with the kid. And Hicks completes the scene by showing William Penn concluding a treaty with the Indians. In proclaiming the peaceable kingdom Jesus is heir to this vision.

Thought for the day

No life form is so humble that it falls outside God's cosmic covenant.

Prayer

Lord of wind and sky, of olive trees and flowing water, help us on this Lenten journey to embrace responsibility for your cosmic covenant. Amen

Fifth Friday of Lent

Who will speak the prophetic word today?

Jer 20:10–13; Ps 18; Jn 10:31–42

We are very close to Holy Week. It is impossible not to feel the tension of the texts. The prophet Jeremiah is threatened with violence on all sides. Jesus manages to escape – for the moment – the stones the Jews will cast at him. But we know his escape is short-lived. So the prophets of history navigate their way through danger trying to articulate the 'fire in the bones', the passion for justice. And they know the cost of discipleship.

But prophecy is not always the lonely task of a vulnerable individual. Recently, by the shores of Lake Galilee, I heard Canon Naim Ateek, of Sabeel, an association that works non-violently for the liberation of Palestinian Christians, remind me that the vocation of the entire Christian community is prophetic. 'You are the salt of the earth,' he exclaimed, 'And the nature of salt is to transform.' The Latin Patriarch, Michel Sabbah, had already urged us – and his words still ring in my ears – that 'Every Christian has a vocation for the Holy Land, a vocation to keep it holy and keep it as a place of redemption.'

Our challenge is to recover fidelity to this challenge. Communities like Taizé, drawing to its hillside thousands of young people each year in search of peace and reconciliation, blaze a torch for us. It is only by coming together that we can recover the prophetic imagination that another world is possible. In this world of instant

76

communication and insatiable global capitalism, we need entire communities of Jeremiahs, not only to be in solidarity with Christians of the Holy Lands, but to bear prophetic witness in lifestyle and in worship that the work of redemption is a vocation for all.

Thought for the day
Another world is possible.

Prayer
Christ our prophet, you witness to God's truth, in fear before the stones they want to throw at you, and in sadness when your chosen friends fail to grasp your message. Grant us the gift together, to see with your prophetic eyes, to act out of your prophetic vision, and to love God's dream of reconciliation with your prophetic heart. Amen

A Covenant of Peace

Ezech 37:21–28; Jer 31:10–13; Jn 11:45–56

Palestine and Israel are still locked in violent dispute, as are the factions within Palestine itself. In Afghanistan the Taliban may be in the ascendant, and there is fierce fighting between factions in Iraq. Closer at home, more prosaically, when the Orthodox composer Sir John Tavener offered a new work in Westminster Cathedral where the names of God as Allah were to be highlighted, a storm of noisy protest was aroused.

And yet, on this, the Eve of Holy Week, we are reminded that God promises a covenant of peace. And this covenant reaches beyond the land of Israel, so that 'the nations will learn that I am the Lord, the sanctifier of Israel'.

Perhaps now, as never before, we understand that the covenant of peace at the heart of the Kingdom proclamation must stretch out beyond Christianity. It must embrace all faiths and all nations. For Jesus the sacrifice demanded was life itself. For us the sacrifice may turn out to be that too, but there are many less dramatic steps before this that must be undergone by every Christian. To understand how God's truth and love is present in the faith of others is the first. To repent of our lack of understanding, our implacable hatred and narrow-mindedness, is the second. And to become aware of how we have negatively altered the course of history in not understanding this universal generosity of God is the third. To embark on this pilgrim journey of new awareness is to prepare ourselves to receive, with great humility, the covenant of peace.

Thought for the day
God is a God of passionate love for all nations

Prayer
God of all nations, we repent of reducing you to the projections of our ambition and selfish desires; as we come in imagination and longing to journey with Jesus in those anguished days towards Calvary, fill our hearts and minds with the vision of your covenant of peace that embraces the nations. Let us, at this moment in history, be committed to your dream for its fulfillment. Amen

Chris Chivers
Holy Week and Easter Sunday

Passion Sunday

All I see is love

Is 50:4–7; Ps 22; Ph 2:6–11; Lk 22:14–23:56

> *'I gave my back to those who struck me … and I know I shall not be put to shame.'* (Isaiah 50:6a, 7b)

When it was released, the film *Shooting Dogs* –set during the terrible events of the Rwandan genocide – was criticised for being yet another movie about African suffering told from the perspective of white people. There's truth in the criticism but somehow the central character, Fr Christopher, a Roman Catholic priest, transcends the limitations of the film-maker's lens. His story can't be summarised in a paragraph. But at its climax, when he has given his all to try and save his people – especially the younger members of his community – he stands facing a man down the barrel of a gun who had but days before been a close associate. Fr Christopher knows that he is about to meet his end. Nothing he can say will stop the man pulling the trigger. He has hate on his heart and it's written all over his face. Yet, in the face of such gratuitous evil, we hear Fr Christopher say simply this: 'When I look into your eyes, all I see is love.'

It's a risky moment in cinematic terms – in theological terms too – because it could see the whole narrative degenerate into sentimentality. But as we look through Fr Christopher's eyes into those of his killer we know that his is no pie in the sky as you die statement. He sees love and for him this is the *imagio dei*, the divine imprint that's there in every soul.

This is the love at the heart of Holy Week. It enables a link to be made, a seeming gap to be filled between a back offered to the smiters and belief that God can ultimately heal the pain of the stripes that are endured. It is love which is costly and transforming. It offers everything on behalf of friend and foe alike. It expects nothing for itself – least of all a 'feel-good-factor' for the giver. This sacrificial 'on behalf of' character – which is so counter-cultural – is the key. This love is self-emptying. It is cross-shaped.

Thought for the day
Love so amazing, so divine, demands my soul, my life, my all. (Isaac Watts)

Prayer
Lord, help me to look at others with a love like your love, and to look at myself with a love as cross-shaped and transforming. Amen

Monday of Holy Week

Aesthetics and ethics

Is 42:1–7; Ps 27; Jn 12:1–11

> 'Why wasn't this perfume not sold for three hundred
> denarii and the money given to the poor?' (John 12:5)

Most of my ministry has been spent in 'cathedrals' –
Cape Town, Westminster Abbey and Blackburn. All of
them in different ways have been places of lavishness. It
was a privilege to direct a project to install 'liberation
panels' into the Great West Window of Cape Town
cathedral to mark South Africa's transformation from
apartheid state to multi-racial democracy. At Westminster Abbey – not a cathedral of course but cathedral-
like nonetheless – I'll never forget my inner gasp when I
caught sight of the crown on top of the Queen Mother's
coffin, or the feeling of elation when the Salvation Army
band marched through the building playing 'Onward
Christian Soldiers' at Dame Thora Hird's Memorial
Service, or the pleasure I derived from working with Will
Tuckett, the choreographer, to bring the English National
Ballet into the building for the very first time. At
Blackburn I enjoy daily Penny Warden's installation, The
Journey, fifteen life-sized paintings which rework the
Stations of the Cross in contemporary terms and narrate
a journey in colour to transform the hardest heart.

But … if I were to tot up the cost of all those memories
it would amount to tens of thousands of pounds. Surely
that money could have been better used? Perhaps. But

such lavishness calls for a comparable super-abundance in response. In Cape Town, we staged orchestral masses once a month and we fed the poorest of the poor in soup kitchen day by day. It was all of a piece. At Blackburn, it's asylum seekers and refugees who benefit daily from the generosity elicited from lovers of the music and the art work. Just as at the Abbey it was the experience of coming out of the Queen Mother's funeral in order to lead a service the same day for survivors of the Rwandan genocide which assured me that the balance was on the right lines. It's easy to be a cynic about lavishness. But there's a connection between aesthetics and ethics which once made proves itself to be utterly life-changing. Mary Magdalene knew this with her pot of nard. Our Lord did too. Of course, lard's more useful a substance, but perhaps not quite so powerful as an agent of transformation.

Thought for the day
'This perpetual fellow led an honest life at Eton; a moderate man whose food was beans; among the virtues in which he shone, he relieved the misery of the poor, and he cultivated music'. (Epitaph on the gravestone of Walter Smythe)

Prayer
Lord, help me to see our great religious buildings
and the creativity that they embody for what they are:
the impetus and inspiration
to assist in the redemption of your world.
Amen

Mandela Christ-light

Is 49:1–6; Ps 71; Jn 13:21–33, 36–38

> *'I will give you as a light to the nations, that my*
> *salvation may reach to the end of the earth.'*
>
> (Isaiah 49:6)

For Holy Week 2007 we invited the South African priest and poet, Harry Wiggett, to Blackburn Cathedral as preacher. Fr Harry had ministered to many of the political prisoners who were household names across the world during the apartheid years. Nelson Mandela recalled, soon after his release from prison, that he had never understood the differences between the four gospels until Fr Harry explained them one day using the table top in the room where a few of Pollsmoor's prisoners met to celebrate together the Eucharist. Fr Harry had invited them to imagine that the table was a soccer field. 'There are four journalists reporting this match,' he had said. 'Each of them has a different perspective when they file their reports. We really wouldn't believe them if they were all the same.' Mandela has treasured that illustration ever since. It clicked for him, as it must have done for others there.

At Blackburn Fr Harry told us of another occasion when he had celebrated the Eucharist at the prison, which he always had to do under the watchful eye of Warder Christo Brandt, the archetypal Afrikaner apartheid functionary, who sat next to the door. Fr Harry had reached the Peace and was just about to share it with the six or so prisoners assembled when Nelson Mandela interrupted the service. Calling over to the warder he said 'Brandt, are you a Christian?' 'Ja, meneer' (Yes, sir), came the reply. 'Well then, you must join us for our service.' Fr Harry admitted that he had never once thought to include Brandt in his monthly Eucharist. But Mandela understood that if he was to fulfil the calling he sensed, to bring healing, reconciliation and restoration he must first set free the oppressor himself, before bringing back the scattered survivors and exiles to a new South Africa.

Mandela knew that his calling was the highest imaginable. He was to be a Christ-light to the nations, a beacon of hope showing a new way of living to all who have the courage to follow.

Thought for the day

> I will hold the Christlight for you
> in the night-time of your fear;
> I will hold my hand out to you,
> Speak the peace you long to hear.
>
> (Richard Gillard)

Prayer

Lord, help us to go the extra mile: not simply to preach to the choir, or wash the feet of those known to us, but to begin your work of transformation with those who seem least likely to respond. Amen

Listening and speaking

Is 50:4–9; Ps 69; Mt 26:14–25

> *'The Lord has given me the tongue of a teacher …*
> *morning by morning he wakens – wakens my ear to*
> *listen as those who are taught.'* (Isaiah 50:4, 5)

A story which has done the rounds for years tells of a priest who when asked why, for several weeks, he had preached the same sermon on the need to love your neighbour, replied: 'I'll stop preaching it when you begin to do it!' There are some sermons that bear much repetition. The verses set for Passion Sunday from Isaiah chapter 50 come round again just three days later because the balance between speaking and listening to which they refer is one with which Christians must wrestle the whole time. There is a Hindu proverb to the effect that we have two ears and only one mouth. It's a brilliant corrective to the missionary monologue that western whites inflicted on their African and Asian sisters and brothers for too long. A monologue, which most often consisted in 'telling the needy what was best for them'.

'When the Nazis came for the Communists, I remained silent; I was not a communist. When they locked up the Social Democrats, I did not speak out; I was not a social democrat. When they came for the Trade Unionists, I did not speak out; I was not a trade unionist. When they came for me, there was no one left to speak out.' Those famous words of Martin Niemöller, one of the founders of the anti-Nazi, Confessing Church, hang over all of us as both challenge and inspiration. But, in the end, we must take our cue from the one who hangs for us on a tree, who speaks to forgive and to comfort, to request and to commend, but whose redeeming love is equally to be felt in the silence.

Thought for the day

Is it true? Is it kind? Is it helpful?

> (Advice before speaking, from Horace Dammers,
> Dean of Bristol, 1973–1986)

Prayer

Lord, help me to know when to be the voice of the voice-less
and when simply to be an actively silent activist
providing the space for their voices – and yours – to be heard.
Amen

How beautiful are your feet?

Ex 2:1–8, 11–14; Ps 16; 1 Cor 11:23–26; Jn 13:1–15

> *'Lord, not my feet only but also my hands and my head!'* (John 13:9)

Seeing me standing on a Cornish beach one day, my wife Mary remarked that she didn't marry me for my feet – or for my money, for that matter. Interestingly, it was the feet on the bodies of peasant pilgrims painted by Caravaggio that incensed one of his patrons. They just weren't respectable enough. They didn't create the right devotional impression. I wonder what this patron would have made of the liturgical washing of feet each Maundy Thursday?

As a teenager I dreaded priests asking me to have my feet washed. So much so that I made sure I was doing something else with them: I took up the organ! I was already conscious that my feet were large and that my toes were somewhat squashed and certainly unattractive to the eye. But as a priest myself – and one who has sometimes met a degree of resistance on the part of those whom he's asked to have their feet washed – I have to say that washing feet is quite one of the most spiritually moving and humbling experiences I've ever had. There's something here in the way in which vulnerability on the part of the washee meets the kneeling humility of the washer.

Feet weren't of course enough for Peter to be going on

with. He wanted Jesus to wash his hands and his head as well. As usual, he missed the point. Since one who's bathed already – in other words, one who's been baptised – doesn't need total immersion in water, just a loving reminder for tired feet of their symbolic importance as the means by which God's message of peace is borne into the world.

Put your own feet up for a few moments and contemplate those of all the Christians world-wide who will walk to church today to begin to accompany Jesus in his lonely trek to the cross. The courage and the contexts involved in making some of these journeys doesn't bear thinking about. Well, actually it does. Think about it now and thank God for all those feet.

Thought for the day
'How beautiful are the feet of them that preach the gospel of peace.' (Romans 10: 15)

Prayer
Lord, help me to walk with you and for you,
to plant my footprints in yours,
and run the way of your commandments.
Amen

Cross-shaped power

Is 52:13–53:12; Ps 31; Heb 4:14–16, 5:7–9; Jn 18:1—19:42

> *Pilate therefore said to him … 'Do you not know I have*
> *power to release you, and power to crucify you?'*
>
> (John 19:10)

Every Good Friday pilgrims walk the length of London's Victoria Street from Methodist Central Hall to Westminster Cathedral and then back towards Westminster Abbey in a Procession of Witness. A heavy cross is borne through the streets to the beat of a lone drum, as Christians of every denomination follow its journey to the point where three hammer blows see the cross set up in the Abbey's nave.

One year, I found myself next to the human rights champion, James Mawdsley, whose story of imprisonment for pro-democracy activities in Burma is movingly documented in his autobiography, *The Heart Must Break*. The book is nothing short of a spiritual classic. The most haunting episode is the moment when he sees his prison warder – a man who has tried to wear down James's spirits in all sorts of petty ways – working in the courtyard beyond his cell. Over the initial weeks of a sentence that could run a twenty-five year course, this man has come to symbolise all that James hates about his Burmese oppressors. But, suddenly, seeing the man silhouetted against the courtyard wall, James realises that this warder is no longer an object of hate but of love. The warder clearly thought that he was the one who held power over James. But James now realised that here was a man much more a victim of oppression than his prisoner. James's innate sense of freedom could never be taken from him. But for this warder there was little prospect of him ever escaping his life as a petty functionary in the oppressive machinery of the Burmese state.

Like Jesus before Pilate, or Gandhi facing the clubs borne by salt-mine guards, or Desmond Tutu standing in Cape Town's Wale Street, the tear gas canisters shooting past his ears, James had realised a fundamental truth, that the only real power there is in the world is cross-shaped. It is the transforming power of sacrificial love.

Thought for the day

Goodness is stronger than evil; love is stronger than hate; light is stronger than darkness; life is stronger than death. Victory is ours through him who loves us.

(Desmond Tutu)

Prayer

Lord, help me never to suppose that I have power over any other human being, save the self-giving power of your Cross. Amen

Waiting and hoping

Gen 1:1–2.2; Is 54:5–14; Mt 28:1–10

> *'Come see the place where he lay.'* (Matthew 28:6b)

In his remarkable book, *Real Presences*, George Steiner commends Holy Saturday to his readers – of whatever faith or none – as the most important day in the life of the world. Given his Jewish roots, this at first seems puzzling. But with remarkable generosity and insight he sees the movement from suffering to hope, that frames the journey from Good Friday to Easter Day, as a movement beyond the specific Christian context in which the story of a crucifixion and a resurrection is rehearsed. In this movement, Holy Saturday is a day of waiting, a day to take seriously the self-emptying character of the cross, a day to focus on the emptiness of a tomb with all its liberating possibilities. It is the day on which we most discern the nature of our humanity because, as RS Thomas once suggested, 'the meaning is in the waiting'.

I found myself early one morning in the Church of the Holy Sepulchre in Jerusalem. The Eucharist was celebrated around the site which – symbolically – has become known as the place of Christ's tomb and hence his resurrection. The ministry of the word was heard in front of the tomb. The Franciscan priest then went inside the tomb to preside over the ministry of the sacrament. As the congregation, we sat facing the place from which the stone had been rolled away. When the priest brought the consecrated bread out of the tomb towards the congregation, I felt I was being commanded to come and see the place where Jesus lay and to accept the reality of his abiding presence in a new way. I dare not refuse to do so. And then having looked and eaten, I, an Anglican priest, was sent out by the Catholic priest into the complexities of a world which, from the perspective of a place like Jerusalem, seem pretty stark. But I'd glimpsed hope before leaving – it had touched my lips and my heart – a hope and strength whose power can still change everything. It had, after all, begun to change me.

Thought for the day
Hope: there is no word less deconstructible.

(George Steiner)

Prayer
Lord, help me to walk the Saturday journey
between suffering and liberation
with a hopefulness that waits with eager longing
and a truthfulness that never loses heart
because it is breaking down all the barriers in your world.
Amen

Loving and eastering

Acts 10:34, 37–43; Ps 118; Col 3:1–4; Jn 20:1–9

'Then the other disciple ... saw and believed'
(John 20: 8)

The fifteen-painting series 'The Journey' by the contemporary artist, Penny Warden, in Blackburn Cathedral
reworks the traditional stations of the cross as a journey
in colour and bodily movement – represents the world of
torture, loneliness and death surrounding the central
protagonist with purples, dark reds, browns and blacks.
But it also contains hints of yellows and oranges
throughout in order to show the sufferer fighting back as
he seeks to overcome whatever is thrown at him. In each
of the paintings, the artist also offers a thoroughly bal-
letic figure, revealed as participant in a dance of death
which becomes – at length – a dance of new life. The
viewer's eyes immediately detect behind her brush-
strokes shadows of distended Ethiopians in the famine of
1985 or the skeletal figures so painfully revealed to the
world in 1945 when the Allies liberated the concentration
camps, the napalm girl from Vietnam running towards
us, the machete-marred bodies of Rwandans strewn
along the roads in Kigali in the 1994 Genocide or the
charred Iraqi in his tank in the 1991 Gulf War.

But paintings speak not just to the eye or even to the
memory. Colour, as Kandinsky asserted, exerts a direct
influence on the soul. And people who walk Penny

Warden's journey in colour, experience it as one by which a victim becomes not just a survivor but actually a victor. You can't fail but to get the point when in the final picture, a wonderful representation of the resurrection, the whole canvas is yellow and orange – with just hints of mauve where nails were once driven – and the dancer pirouettes exuberantly from the tomb. But only one child – after the paintings had been installed for six months – noticed that around this figure the artist had made some 'splashes' that form the shape of a heart. 'What does that mean?' I said to her. 'Loving', she replied, adding almost by accident as she continued to think aloud, '... easter-ing.' 'Yes,' I thought. 'You're so right ... Easter's much more verb than noun.'

So to the task we share with God of eastering the world ...

Thought for the day

'Let him easter in us, be a dayspring to the dimness of us, be a crimson-crested east.'

(from 'The Wreck of the Deutschland',
Gerald Manley Hopkins)

Prayer

Lord, easter in me
the reality of your transforming love,
that changing the landscape within
I may work with you to transfigure the world without
with the colours and the dancing of your eternal kingdom.
Amen

CAFOD is the Catholic Agency for Overseas Development. It is the official overseas development and relief agency of the Catholic Church in England and Wales. CAFOD has been fighting poverty in developing countries since 1962.

CAFOD believes that all human beings have a right to dignity and respect, and that the world's resources are a gift to be shared equally by all men and women, whatever their race, nationality or religion.

CAFOD is a member of the Caritas International Federation, a worldwide network of Catholic relief and development organisations.

CAFOD raises funds from the Catholic community in England and Wales, the UK government and the general public so that it can:

- promote long-term development, helping people in need to bring about change for themselves through development and relief work.
- respond to emergencies, providing immediate help for people affected by conflict or natural disasters.
- identify the causes of poverty and raise public awareness of them, encouraging supporters and the public to challenge the structures, policies and attitudes that reinforce inequality.
- speak out on behalf of poor communities, explaining the underlying causes of poverty and challenging governments and international bodies to adopt policies that promote equality and justice.

- promote human development and social justice in witness to Christian faith and gospel values.

Enacting Gospel values

CAFOD's work is one of the ways in which the Church expresses and enacts its belief in human dignity and social justice.

It is inspired by Scripture ('to bring good news to the poor,' Luke 4:18), by Catholic Social Teaching and by the experiences and hopes of the poor, marginalised and often oppressed communities it supports.

It works to enact Gospel values – within and beyond the Church – including:

- concern for our neighbours and the wellbeing of future generations
- serving the common good to enable everyone to develop equally
- fighting for social justice and ensuring everyone's basic needs are met
- acting on the basis of need, not greed, and acting in solidarity with those living in poverty
- promoting the values of human dignity, community, stewardship and the integrity of creation.

CAFOD puts into practice the solidarity and communion for which the Church stands, and strives for a world built on interdependence, mutuality and sharing, where exclusion, exploitation and greed do not exist.

Website: www.cafod.org.uk

About Christian Aid

In 1945, the British and Irish churches created Christian Aid to put faith into action amid the ruins of a horrific war. Sixty years on, we work with church partners, the ecumenical family and sister agencies as well as with alliances of other faiths and secular groups which share our passionate determination to end poverty.

Christian Aid works wherever the need is greatest – irrespective of religion or race.

Because we believe in strengthening people to find their own solutions to the problems they face, we support local organisations, which are best placed to understand local needs. We also give help on the ground through 16 overseas offices.

Christian Aid Week each year is the largest house-to-house collection in the UK, with the involvement of over 300,000 volunteers and 20,000 local churches and committees.

We strive for a new world transformed by an end to poverty and we campaign to change the rules that keep people poor.

Our values

The essential purpose of Christian Aid is to expose the scandal of poverty, to help in practical ways to root it out from the world, and to challenge and change the systems which favour the rich and powerful over the poor and marginalised.

Put life first
We believe that all people are created equal, with inherent dignity and infinite worth. Individual human needs must always come first, ahead of dogma, ideology or political necessity. We know that each one of us, in all our diversity and varied talents, can make a real difference in the battle to end poverty and injustice.

Struggle for justice
Poverty is a condition created by an unjust society, denying people access to, and control over, the resources they need to live a full life.

So we take the side of poor and marginalised people as they struggle to realise their civil, political, economic, social and cultural rights.

We believe in the just and sustainable use of the earth and its resources, so that the greed of one generation will not create poverty for the next.

Speak out courageously
We have a duty to speak out and act with conviction to challenge and change the systems that create poverty.

Christian Aid always remains independent of governments and other powerful institutions. We work to educate and mobilise people from all kinds of backgrounds to build a global movement which can change the course of history.

Test everything against experience
We know that poor people are the true experts on the nature of poverty, and our work is shaped by their voices and concerns.

In a spirit of humility, we try to learn from our own mistakes and from the experience of those we work alongside, to improve the impact of our work.

We know that lasting solutions can never be imposed on communities from the outside.

Work together with others
All our work is based on the spirit of cooperation and partnership. We help to build a world free from poverty through inter-faith and intercommunity dialogue and cooperation.

We nurture the talents, commitment and energy of all our supporters, volunteers and staff. Together we uphold a commitment to honesty, mutual respect, accountability and diversity.

Towards a new earth
For Christian Aid this is a time to act upon our dream of a new earth on which we all stand equally, to renew our faith and hope, to reaffirm our commitment to the world's poorest communities, and to promote the dignity and rights of people throughout the world.

Website: www.christian-aid.org.uk